The KidHaven Science Library

Tsunamis

by Peggy J. Parks

KIDHAVEN PRESS

An imprint of Thomson Gale, a part of The Thomson Corporation

THOMSON

GALE

Detroit • New York • San Francisco • San Diego • New Haven, Conn. • Waterville, Maine • London • Munich

© 2006 Thomson Gale, a part of The Thomson Corporation.

Thomson and Star Logo are trademarks and Gale and KidHaven Press are registered trademarks used herein under license.

For more information, contact
KidHaven Press
27500 Drake Rd.
Farmington Hills, MI 48331-3535
Or you can visit our Internet site at http://www.gale.com

LIBRARY OF CONGRESS CATALOGING-IN-PUBLICATION DATA

Parks, Peggy J., 1951–
    Tsunamis / by Peggy J. Parks.
        p. cm. — (The Kidhaven science library)
Includes bibliographical references.
ISBN 0-7377-3380-2 (hard cover : alk. paper)
1. Tsunamis—Juvenile literature.   I. Title. II. Series.
GC221.5P37 2005
551.46'37--dc22
                                                                        2005009015

Printed in the United States of America

Contents

"I Thought It Was the End of the World"

No one expected disaster to strike on December 26, 2004. The Indian Ocean was calm and the sun was brilliant in the clear blue sky. Beaches along the coastline were filled with tourists. They were enjoying the beautiful day, splashing in the water and basking in the sun. Then suddenly the sea began to change.

Journalist Michael Dobbs was swimming in the ocean by Sri Lanka, an island country off the coast of India. His brother, who was closer to shore, began shouting at Dobbs: "Come back! Come back! There's something strange happening with the sea."[1] Dobbs was confused because the ocean was as smooth as glass—and then he saw what his brother meant. Even though there were barely any ripples on the surface of the water, the sea was rising fast. In less than one minute, it rose 15 feet (4.6m). It rushed back out as fast as it had appeared, and then a massive wall of water slammed into the coastline. A deadly natural phenomenon known as a **tsunami** had struck.

The Angry Sea

Tsunamis are some of nature's most destructive forces. They are formed when Earth is shaken by violent disturbances such as underwater earthquakes. When a severe quake strikes deep beneath the ocean floor, massive shock waves travel through the water. The shock waves create a huge surge of seawater known as a **swell**—and a deadly tsunami is born.

Much like the ripples from a stone dropped in a pond, the tsunami's waves begin to spread rapidly in all directions. They continue moving outward away from the **epicenter**, or source of the earthquake. The waves merge with other waves, forming **wave trains** that can stretch for hundreds of miles. They roar across the ocean, gaining strength and speed along the way. When they reach land, they strike forcefully with little or no warning.

An underwater earthquake triggered the December 2004 tsunami. The earthquake occurred about 4 miles (6.4km) beneath the Indian Ocean, off the coast of the Indonesian island of Sumatra. A fisherman in India named Baalaramanan, who witnessed the tsunami, describes what he saw: "That morning, the sea was like it always is. Then suddenly it was on fire. Boiling. It lifted up 11 yards

Satellite photos show the initial tsunami wave rushing away from a beach in Sri Lanka (above). Within minutes, the deadly wave slams into the shoreline (below).

[10m] and paused, almost like it was surveying us below it. And then it fell. It consumed one house after another, like paper boxes."[2] Baalaramanan survived by clinging to a coconut tree as the water raged beneath him and, flooded the land.

Tragic Aftermath

The incident described by Baalaramanan was just one of thousands. The tsunami pounded the coastlines of eleven countries from Thailand to Africa. Wherever it struck, death and destruction were left in its wake. Untold numbers of buildings, including homes, shops, hotels, churches, and schools were destroyed by the raging waters. The tsunami snapped huge trees in two like twigs. It smashed fishing boats to bits and tossed automobiles into hotel lobbies. It derailed trains, flipping over their cars or propelling them into buildings. The floods swept buses filled with passengers out to sea.

Millions of people were left homeless by the tsunami. But the greatest tragedy was the vast number of people who were killed. Because of the number of lives lost, this tsunami was the worst ever recorded in history. About 300,000 people were reported dead or missing. The tsunami hit Indonesia the hardest, especially the province of Aceh. Entire communities were literally washed away. On Sumatra the tsunami left the streets of Meulaboh littered with bodies.

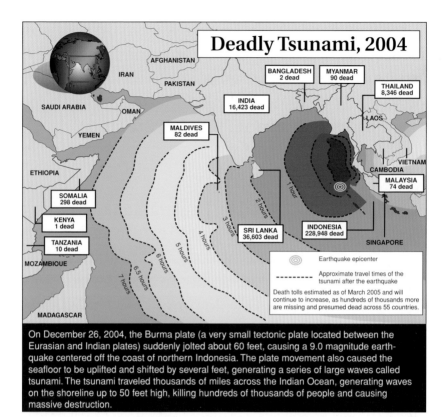

Deadly Tsunami, 2004

AFGHANISTAN

IRAN

PAKISTAN

BANGLADESH
2 dead

MYANMAR
90 dead

THAILAND
8,346 dead

SAUDI ARABIA

OMAN

INDIA
16,423 dead

LAOS

YEMEN

MALDIVES
82 dead

VIETNAM

ETHIOPIA

CAMBODIA

MALAYSIA
74 dead

SOMALIA
298 dead

1 hour

2 hours

KENYA
1 dead

3 hours

SRI LANKA
36,603 dead

INDONESIA
228,948 dead

SINGAPORE

TANZANIA
10 dead

4 hours

5 hours

MOZAMBIQUE

6 hours

6.5 hours

7 hours

MADAGASCAR

◎ Earthquake epicenter

- - - - - Approximate travel times of the
tsunami after the earthquake

Death tolls estimated as of March 2005 and will
continue to increase, as hundreds of thousands more
are missing and presumed dead across 55 countries.

On December 26, 2004, the Burma plate (a very small tectonic plate located between the Eurasian and Indian plates) suddenly jolted about 60 feet, causing a 9.0 magnitude earthquake centered off the coast of northern Indonesia. The plate movement also caused the seafloor to be uplifted and shifted by several feet, generating a series of large waves called tsunami. The tsunami traveled thousands of miles across the Indian Ocean, generating waves on the shoreline up to 50 feet high, killing hundreds of thousands of people and causing massive destruction.

A resident of the city, Nurjamin Samsinar, shares: "We thought it wasn't possible that the ocean could flood the town. But when the second wave came, it was huge, twice the size of the mosque. . . . I thought it was the end of the world."[3]

Caught Off Guard

Experts say the Southeast Asia tsunami did not have to have such a tragic ending. They believe so many people died because they were completely unprepared. If they had known a tsunami was on its way, people in some areas could have escaped to higher ground. Thousands of lives might have been saved.

A system for monitoring tsunamis exists for the Pacific Ocean, but there is no such system in Southeast Asia. That is largely because tsunamis are extremely rare in the Indian Ocean. Scientists at the Pacific Tsunami Warning Center (PTWC) in Hawaii forecast the tsunami within minutes of the earthquake. They wanted to warn people in Asia, but they were not sure whom to contact. A warning was e-mailed to some coastal nations, including Indonesia and Thailand. However, officials in those countries did not receive the communication in time.

Nature's Warning

The tsunami actually sent a warning of its own, but few people knew how to read the signs. One characteristic of tsunamis is that they often hit the shore

An SUV sits on top of an enormous pile of rubble near a coastal mosque in Banda Aceh, Indonesia, after the tsunami hit.

at different intervals. After the first wave strikes, the water rushes back out to sea. That is what happened in Thailand and Sri Lanka. The first wave hit and then quickly receded, leaving bays empty and large parts of the seafloor exposed. Fishing boats were stranded on the sand. Scores of brilliantly colored fish flopped helplessly on the shore. Because the mysterious wave was gone, people assumed the danger was over. Thousands of curious onlookers, including many children, rushed down to the beaches to get a closer look. Tourists wandered around snapping photographs. These people had no idea that a disaster was just minutes away.

The day after the tsunami struck, dead fish litter the beach near a stranded fishing boat in Penang, Malaysia.

But those who were knowledgeable about the sea suspected that a tsunami was on the way. One of them was a man from India's Nicobar Islands. He had learned about tsunamis by watching a television documentary. When he saw what was happening to the ocean, he sounded an alarm. Then he led his fellow villagers to higher ground. As a result, he saved the lives of 1,500 people. More lives were saved at a luxury resort in Phuket, Thailand. An employee noticed that the water level had drastically dropped. Sensing that something was wrong, he called his boss, who told him a tsunami was about to strike. The two men warned people to get away from the beach. Five minutes later, powerful waves struck the shore.

A Sixth Sense?

Amazingly enough, animals were better prepared for the approaching disaster than humans. Witnesses reported that animals behaved very strangely about an hour before the tsunami struck. People at a wildlife reserve in Sri Lanka saw three elephants run away from the beach. Flamingos abandoned low-lying breeding areas and flew to higher ground. Many other types of animals stayed far away from the shore.

After the tsunami, a news photographer flew over the Sri Lanka park in a helicopter. He observed abundant wildlife, including elephants, buffalo, and deer. He did not, however, see even one animal

Scientists believe that the acute senses of many animals, such as these deer in India, drove them to seek shelter long before the tsunami hit.

corpse. Experts say that the animals' acute senses may have alerted them that danger was approaching. Wildlife scientist Alan Rabinowitz explains: "Earthquakes bring vibrational changes on land and in water. . . . Some animals have acute sense of hearing and smell that allow them to determine something coming towards them long before humans might know that something is there."[4]

Tsunamis are dangerous natural phenomena. They do not occur very often, and are especially rare in the Indian Ocean. But on December 26, 2004, people learned just how deadly they can be. As the death toll continues to rise, the Southeast Asia tsunami of 2004 may well become known as the worst disaster of all time.

Chapter 2

A Raging Wall of Water

Tsunamis are made of the most powerful waves on Earth. Like normal waves, they have a **crest** (the highest point) and a **trough** (the lowest point). But as journalist Daniel Pendick explains, the resemblance ends there: "Though it's true that tsunamis are ocean waves, calling them by the same name as the ordinary wind-driven variety is a bit like referring to firecrackers and atomic warheads both as 'explosives.'"[5]

Not Just Any Wave

One major difference between waves is how they form. Normal waves are usually the products of wind. Their size and strength depend on how strong the wind blows. But the wind has nothing to do with tsunamis. Shock waves deep within the Earth create them.

Another difference is wave height. Wind-driven waves form on the surface of the water. Their height

After venturing far out when the water initially receded, tourists in Thailand run for shore as the first tsunami waves hit.

is measured from the surface upward. In the open ocean, where gale-force winds are common, wind-driven waves may grow to be 90 feet (27.4m) tall. Tsunami waves, however, do not look like much of anything in the open ocean. Sometimes they are merely ripples that are barely noticeable above the waterline. Sailors or fishermen out in the ocean could watch a deadly tsunami pass right by and never even be aware of it. But tsunami waves are dangerously deceptive—and enormous. They begin deep beneath the ocean's surface and stretch upward from the seafloor. So their true height is often thousands of feet.

Tsunamis also differ from normal waves because of their **wavelength**, which is how far the waves spread out across the ocean. The average wavelength of wind-driven waves is from 300 to 600 feet (100 to 200m). Tsunami waves stretch over great distances that often cover hundreds of miles.

Speed and Force

Tsunamis gather tremendous strength when they are in the deepest part of the ocean. Also, the deeper the water, the faster they can move. Tsunamis can zoom across the ocean as fast as 600 miles per hour (965kph). That is an amazing speed—about as fast as a jet can fly!

Because of the tremendous power behind them, tsunamis retain most of their energy even as they travel great distances. For instance, in May 1960 an earthquake struck near the coast of Chile. The quake generated a deadly tsunami. After devastating Chilean coastal areas, it roared across the Pacific Ocean. Within fifteen hours the tsunami had reached the coast of Hawaii. Even after traveling 6,200 miles (10,000km), it was still forceful enough to kill 61 people and destroy millions of dollars in property. Yet the tsunami did not stop there. About seven hours later, it arrived in Japan—which is 10,000 miles (16,000km) from where it began. There it took more than 100 lives. Pendick describes the behavior of this type of tsunami: "The waves from a trans-Pacific tsunami can reverberate back and forth across the ocean for days, making it jiggle like a planetary-scale pan of Jell-O."[6]

In May 1960, a Japanese family gets a close look at a fishing boat that was heaved out of the water by a tsunami.

Coastal Catastrophes

As a tsunami gets closer to land, it goes through a huge change. First, the shallower water causes it to slow down—and then the real danger begins. The energy stored within the tsunami compresses and increases the power of the waves. The front wave slows down first. Then all the waves behind it scrunch together like cars crashing in a freeway pileup. This causes the tsunami to heave upward, forming waves as high as 100 feet (30m). The tower of water thunders toward the coastline anywhere from 30 to 100 miles (72 to 160km) per hour. It can strike with a terrifying force, sweeping away everything in its path. Journalist Michael Elliott explains: "It crashes onto shore with the power to wreck buildings and throw trucks around as if they were Ping-Pong balls."[7]

When a fierce Pacific Ocean tsunami slammed into Alaska's Aleutian Islands in 1946, it caused this type of catastrophic damage. The tsunami's waves were so massive that the Scotch Cap Lighthouse was destroyed. This was no small structure. It was five stories high and reinforced with steel. Even though it stood 35 feet (10m) above sea level, the tsunami blasted the lighthouse into a pile of rubble.

Tourists and residents of the town of Koh Raya, Thailand, flee as an enormous wave crashes onto shore.

The greatest risks during a tsunami are to areas within 1 mile (1.6km) of a coastline. The debris that is propelled through raging floodwaters poses serious danger. Cars, trucks, boats, and other large objects can move through the water at frightening speed. People hit by the debris can be seriously injured or even crushed to death.

The flooding itself poses another grave danger. Michael Dobbs says that after the tsunami hit Sri Lanka in 2004, homes in the coastal villages immediately filled with water. He explains: "As the water rushed out of the bay, I scrambled onto the main road. Screams were coming from the houses beyond the road, many of which were still half full of water that had trapped the inhabitants inside."[8] Dobbs's brother's house, built on a rock 60 feet (18m) above sea level, was untouched by the tsunami. Hundreds of other homes, however, were completely washed away.

Can the Land Recover?

The powerful forces at work during a tsunami can radically change the landscape. The tsunami of 2004 caused severe flooding over thousands of miles. In some instances, the water surged into coastal areas 1,000 feet (305m) or more. Some experts think the flooding could cause permanent changes to the land.

One country where this is a concern is India. Some scientists fear that India's Andaman and

In Sri Lanka, tsunami waves flood low-lying houses, many with people still trapped inside.

Nicobar islands may have been permanently changed by the tsunami. The coast guard surveyed the islands from above. Officials confirmed that one of the islands appears to have split in two. Another looks like it was chopped into three sections. A third island, called North Sentinel Island and home to the Sentinelese, also appears to be reshaped. A local coast guard commander named Anil Pokhariyal explains: "A long stretch of coral reef, which used to be under the sea, has now emerged overland. The island appears to have tilted—one side submerged and the other emerging above water."[9]

After the Chilean tsunami in 1960, pine plantations became nothing more than salt marshes. Chileans had grown the pine trees for timber, and

An Indonesian man who lost his wife and home in the tsunami surveys the ruins of his town.

planted them in low-lying areas. The earthquake that caused the tsunami lowered the ground even farther. When seawater flooded the plantation, the ground became too wet and salty for the trees to survive. This happened in other areas of Chile as well. Salty seawater flooded coastal pastures, farms, and forests, ruining the land for growing any sort of vegetation.

Tsunamis are unlike any other force in nature. They are composed of immensely powerful waves that are fueled by energy from deep in Earth. They have the power to wipe out coastlines, crumble buildings, and destroy entire cities. The scars they leave behind are devastating reminders of how vicious nature can be. Whether those scars are temporary or permanent can only be known through the passing of time.

Chapter 3

Disasters of Nature

It takes an extremely violent force to create tsunamis. About 95 percent of them are caused by underwater earthquakes. The earthquake that struck Southeast Asia in December 2004 measured more than 9.0 on the **Richter scale** (a system of calculating earthquake activity). It was the worst earthquake in 40 years. In fact, it was so powerful that very few earthquakes in history can even compare.

Earth's Shifting Crust

To understand why earthquakes cause tsunamis, it is necessary to examine the natural forces behind them. Earthquakes are almost always caused by the shifting of Earth's continents. This shifting is explained by **plate tectonics**. Plate tectonics is based on a scientific theory that Earth's crust is divided into about a dozen gigantic chunks, or plates. They float on the mantle, which is a churning layer of molten rock. The plates are never still. They constantly move and shift. Science writer Joseph B. Verrengia explains: "The crust is not solid

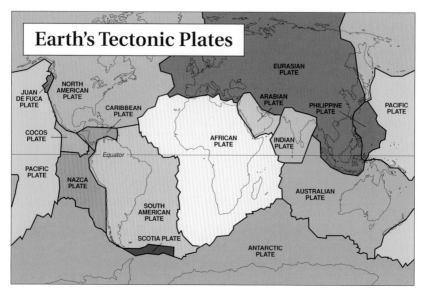

Earth's Tectonic Plates

and unbroken like the coating on a gumball. Rather, it is fractured into more than a dozen overlapping, rigid plates of rocky armor. The plates move relative to one another as they slide atop the hotter layers below."[10]

The fractures in the crust are called **fault lines**, or **faults**. These are the areas where the plates meet. Sometimes they just slide by each other. Other times they head straight toward each other and collide. When this happens, lighter plates are shoved under heavier ones. Severe collisions can cause large earthquakes.

Earthquakes that trigger tsunamis occur beneath the ocean floor. The Southeast Asia earthquake of 2004 was caused by a collision between the India and Burma plates. They join together under the Indian Ocean, connected by a fault line that is about 750 miles (1,207km) long. These two plates have been crunching together for centuries. In the process, the India plate has been pushing its way under the Burma plate. This has happened very gradually, though. The plates typically move about 2.5 inches (6.4cm) per year—about twice as fast as fingernails grow.

But on December 26 the movement was massive and abrupt. Forces had been building up deep in Earth for hundreds of years. Finally, the stress became so strong that it snapped the Burma plate. This caused the seafloor to rupture, and the result was a violent underwater explosion. Trillions of tons of rock shot upward with tremendous force. This released an enormous amount of energy—as much as several thousand nuclear bombs. All that energy transferred to the water generated the tsunami.

Alaskan Catastrophe

As powerful as that earthquake was, the one that struck in Alaska in 1964 was even more powerful. Known as the Good Friday Earthquake, it was the largest ever recorded in the Northern Hemisphere and the second largest in history. It happened on the evening of March 27, 14 miles (22.58km) below the Gulf of Alaska. The shock waves triggered a tsunami that raced toward the mainland. Writer Douglas James Gates describes the chaos that followed: "Unable to remain standing due to the

Inside a Tsunami

①

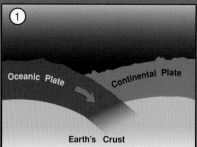

Most large tsunamis result from tectonic earthquakes. Extreme pressure builds when oceanic and continental plates press together. Eventually the heavier oceanic plate slips under the lighter continental plate and causes an underwater earthquake.

②

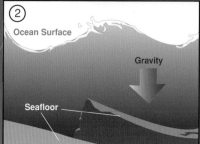

The earthquake lifts part of the ocean floor up and drops other parts down. What happens on the seafloor is mirrored on the ocean surface above. Then gravity acts fast to quickly even out the water surface.

③

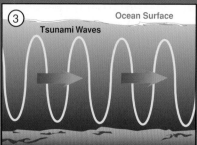

Even though the ocean surface looks flat, waves are moving through the ocean at speeds up to 600 miles per hour. Tsunami waves carry a lot of energy and can extend thousands of feet deep. Tsunami waves also move a lot of water, so they can sometimes travel 10,000 miles or more.

④

When tsunami waves get close to shore they do not have the room they need to keep moving, so they slow down and pack together. Compacted waves cause the ocean to swell, forming a wall of water with a lot of energy inside.

⑤

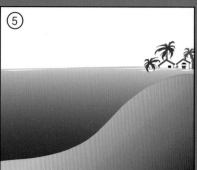

Depending on the shape of the seafloor, the approaching tsunami will most often resemble a rapidly rising tide.

⑥

But some coastlines can slow the tsunami down enough to push it upward into a massive wave or series of waves, which is what happened in South Asia.

seismic [earthquake-produced] waves that were hurling anything and everything into the air, people clung to lamp posts, cars, and each other in an attempt to keep from being knocked down."[11] The tsunami's waves were more than 100 feet (31m) high—as tall as a ten-story building.

The tsunami's first victim was the Alaskan port town of Valdez. The entire coastline was washed away. A large freighter docked there, called the SS *Chena*, was overpowered by massive waves. The ship flipped over onto its side. The tsunami slammed the *Chena* onto dry land and then returned to sweep it back out to sea. Thirty people standing on the dock drowned, as did three who were on the ship. By the time the tsunami had finished pounding the Alaskan coast, a total of 114 people were dead.

Yet the devastation was not confined to Alaska. The earthquake also generated another tsunami in the Pacific Ocean. It traveled as far away as Canada and the Hawaiian Islands, and then moved on to the coasts of Oregon and California. The tsunami caused death and destruction in those areas too. It took the lives of eleven people from Crescent City, California, nearly 2,000 miles (3,200km) from where the tsunami began.

Exploding Mountains

Although earthquakes are responsible for most tsunamis, there are other causes. For example, volcanic eruptions can trigger a tsunami. The greatest risk is from volcanoes that are beneath the ocean floor or on the water's edge. Violent eruptions can send tons of rock, ash, and molten lava pouring into the ocean. Volcanoes also release gases into the sea, which create tremendous underwater pressure. Together these forces can displace immense amounts of seawater and generate a tsunami.

In 1883 a tsunami resulted from the eruption of Krakatoa, a volcano on the Indonesian island of Rakata. Krakatoa had been inactive for more than 200 years. When it finally erupted, the explosion was violent. The volcano blasted steam, ash, and fire nearly 7 miles (11km) into the atmosphere. As far as 75 miles (120km) away, sailors on a ship could see the black clouds of smoke rising above the volcano.

Krakatoa's eruption shook nearly the entire planet. The force of the explosion triggered not just one tsunami but a whole series of them. Some of the waves towered more than 120 feet (40m). They raged through the islands of Java and Sumatra. Nearly 300 towns and villages were destroyed and more than 36,000 people were killed.

Dangers from Space

Another potential tsunami risk comes not from Earth but from space. Comets and asteroids have regularly struck the planet throughout its history. For instance, in 1908 a large comet exploded over

An illustration shows the eruption of Krakatoa in 1883 that sent smoke and ash high into the air and generated a series of tsunamis.

a remote area in Siberia. Witnesses said the sky seemed to split apart and was ablaze with fire. Because not many people lived in the area, there were few deaths. But scientists say that if the comet had struck the ocean rather than land, it would have caused a deadly tsunami.

A pebble thrown into a pond creates ripples on the water's surface. In the same way, an asteroid that crashed into the ocean would generate tsunamis.

An asteroid striking Earth would most likely land in the ocean. That is because nearly three-fourths of the planet's surface is covered by water. The fiery object would blast through the water and crash into the seabed below. Science writer Michael Paine explains how this could lead to a tsunami: "A gigantic explosion occurs and the asteroid is pulverised and vaporised, along with a huge volume of water. This creates a crater in the water surface that quickly fills. The filling process generates a series of tsunamis that radiate across the ocean. The effect is similar to a pebble thrown into a pond, though with a 50,000-mph [80,000-kph] impact, we're not talking ripples here."[12]

Scientists at the Los Alamos National Laboratory in New Mexico have made calculations about such an occurrence. They say that if an asteroid 3 miles (4.83km) across hit the middle of the Atlantic Ocean, a powerful tsunami would be triggered. Waves would pound the upper East Coast of the United States, including New York City. The tsunami would also head in other directions, likely flooding the coasts of France and Portugal. No such catastrophe has ever occurred, but some scientists insist that the risk is very real.

Tsunamis do not just happen on their own. They begin with violent disturbances in Earth, most commonly with underwater earthquakes. No matter what causes them to form, tsunamis are a reminder of just how deadly ocean waves can be.

Chapter 4

Sounding the Alarm

Because tsunamis are products of nature, they cannot be prevented. However, scientists continue to study them extensively. Their goal is to learn more about what triggers tsunamis and how they behave once they form. Understanding their causes and characteristics will help scientists develop better ways to predict tsunamis and educate the public about them.

Learning from the Past

Scientists have gained valuable knowledge from the disastrous December 2004 tsunami. In January 2005 teams of researchers traveled to countries on the Indian Ocean. They wanted to study the physical effects of the tsunami before nature erased the evidence. Of particular interest to scientists is **inundation**, or how far a tsunami travels inland. Killed vegetation and scattered debris provided them with many clues about inundation. To estimate **run-up**, or the maximum height of the waves, scientists examined debris that had been swept onto the tops of trees. They also studied sand and other **sediments** washed ashore during the tsunami. These deposits provided more clues about wave heights. They also helped scientists determine the tsunami's velocity, or its approximate speed and force when it struck the coastline.

When studying sediments from a recent tsunami, scientists may also find deposits left over from tsunamis of the past. These can show how often tsunamis have occurred in a particular area. Ancient sediments also provide clues about the likelihood of future tsunamis in the area. U.S. Geological Survey (USGS) scientist Bruce Jaffe was part of a

After being washed out to sea by the tsunami, this train in Sri Lanka was swept inland and came to rest on top of a grove of trees.

team that spent time in Sri Lanka in early 2005. He explains the value of studying sediment deposits: "The sedimentary record of tsunamis may provide the best evidence of a region's risk from tsunamis."[13]

Scientists have learned that tsunamis behave differently based on variations in the land. For example, waves are highest along shorelines that directly face a tsunami's approach. The slope of the ocean floor can also influence wave activity. Where there is a steep drop-off from the coastline to the open sea, a natural barrier is formed. The barrier can tame the waves, making them less fierce when they reach the shoreline. Another influential factor is coral reefs. Large offshore reefs can buffer waves before they reach the coastline.

By studying how the shape of the land influences tsunami behavior, scientists have found that nature is responsible for a lot of the damage—but not all of it. Humans also share the blame. For example, people removed a high sand dune in Sri Lanka to improve the ocean view at a resort. When the tsunami struck the island in 2004, some areas were harder hit than others. The waves could not pass through the beaches where the dune was still standing. But in areas where the dune had been removed, the situation was quite different, as scientist Bob Morton explains: "Where the dune was gone, the tsunami roared right through."[14] Because humans had altered the land, a hotel was demolished and more than 175 people were killed.

A man surveys the damage after the tsunami ravaged the town of Hut Bay on the Andaman and Nicobar islands in India.

Guarding Coastlines

Even though scientists cannot stop tsunamis, technology can help them save lives. Monitoring and warning systems protect people in many coastal countries. The Pacific Tsunami Warning Center in Hawaii watches over the Hawaiian Islands and other American territories in the Pacific. It also serves as the International Tsunami Information Center for 25 other Pacific Ocean countries. The West Coast/Alaska Tsunami Warning Center is located in Palmer, Alaska. It monitors **seismic** activity in Alaska, British Columbia, Washington, Oregon, and California.

These systems are composed of several elements that work together. **Seismographs** monitor earth-

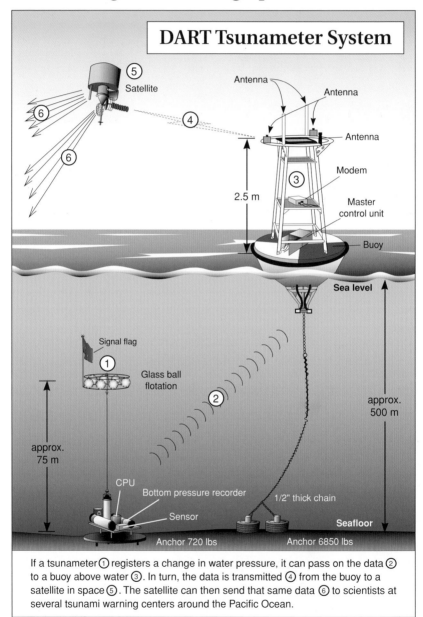

DART Tsunameter System

If a tsunameter ① registers a change in water pressure, it can pass on the data ② to a buoy above water ③. In turn, the data is transmitted ④ from the buoy to a satellite in space ⑤. The satellite can then send that same data ⑥ to scientists at several tsunami warning centers around the Pacific Ocean.

quake activity. They alert scientists if an earthquake is strong enough to produce a tsunami. Tidal gauges record changes in ocean depth. They are used to determine whether a tsunami is actually on its way.

A highly sophisticated tsunami-detecting system was developed by the U.S. National Oceanic and Atmospheric Administration. The system features Deep Ocean Assessment and Reporting of Tsunamis (DART) sensors. These are deep-sea pressure detectors that measure changes in water depth as a tsunami passes overhead. The heart of the system is bottom-pressure recorders that are anchored to the ocean floor. They monitor water pressure and sea level. The instruments are so sensitive that they can detect the tiniest changes in pressure. They can also sense a rise in sea level of just ½ inch (1cm). When they sense change, they relay the information to large high-tech buoys that float above them on the ocean surface. The buoys have Global Positioning System (GPS) antennas mounted on top. They transmit the data to satellites, which in turn send signals to regional warning centers.

One of the most advanced systems in the world is in Japan, where earthquakes and tsunamis are common. Journalist Mark Simkin explains: "Japan knows the cost of tsunamis all too well. The word means 'harbour wave' in Japanese and tsunamis have claimed thousands of lives here in the last century."[15] The Japan Meteorological Society runs the Tsunami Warning Service. The service's technology is so sophisticated that it can predict the height, speed, destination, and arrival time of any tsunami headed for Japan's shores.

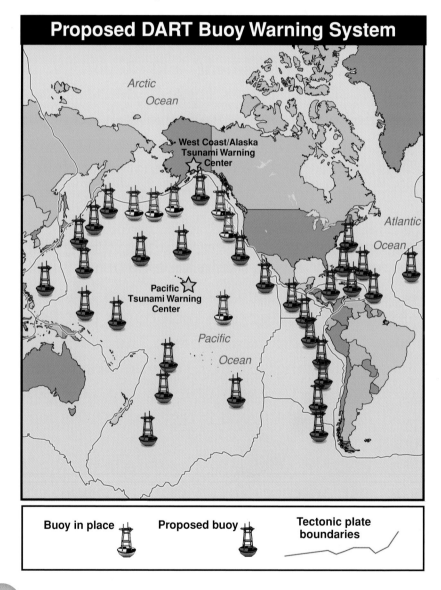

Proposed DART Buoy Warning System

Arctic Ocean

West Coast/Alaska Tsunami Warning Center

Atlantic Ocean

Pacific Tsunami Warning Center

Pacific Ocean

Buoy in place   Proposed buoy   Tectonic plate boundaries

A Worldwide Need

In the past, warning systems such as these were limited to countries along the Pacific Ocean. That is where earthquakes and tsunamis are most likely to occur. But the tragedies of the 2004 tsunami captured the world's attention. It became obvious that such technology was needed to protect countries in Southeast Asia as well. To accomplish this, representatives from more than 50 countries met in Thailand in January 2005. Additional meetings were held in Japan and Paris to plan a tsunami warning system for the Indian Ocean and Southeast Asia. With worldwide cooperation, the system will be in place by mid-2006 or early 2007.

But scientists warn that technology alone cannot prevent another disaster. Educating the public about tsunamis is equally important. According to Waverly Person, a scientist with the USGS, people need to understand the warning signs. He says that in countries along the Indian Ocean, people had no idea that a tsunami was on its way. At the first tremors of the earthquake, they should have gotten away from the shore and run for higher ground. But because they knew nothing about tsunamis, they did not know what to expect or what to do. "People along the Japanese coasts, along the coasts of California, are taught to move away from the coasts," he says. "But a lot of these people in the area where this occurred, they probably had no

In an effort to prevent future tragedies, scientists like this one at the Pacific Tsunami Warning Center are working to improve early-warning systems.

kind of lessons or any knowledge of tsunamis because they are so rare."[16]

Australian scientist Phil McFadden agrees that education is just as crucial as the warning system itself. He says people must be told what to do when an alarm is sounded: "If it's a tsunami, you've got to get the information down to the last Joe on the beach. This is the stuff that is really very hard."[17] Bill McGuire, a scientist with a research center in London, explains that concept even further: "There has to be an effective and efficient communications cascade from the warning centre to the fisherman on the beach and his family and the bar owners."[18]

Looking Toward the Future

Just as scientists cannot prevent earthquakes and volcanoes, they do not have the power to stop tsunamis. They can, however, use technology to save lives. Sophisticated instruments monitor seismic activity and help scientists assess whether tsunamis are likely to occur. Seafloor sensors and high-tech buoys monitor water pressure and sea level. As technology continues to be perfected, the world's monitoring and warning systems will become even more accurate and precise. These systems, combined with improved communication and education, may mean the tragic outcome of the 2004 tsunami will never be repeated.

Chapter 1: "I Thought It Was the End of the World"

1. Quoted in Michael Dobbs, "It Seemed Like a Scene from the Bible," Washingtonpost.com, December 27, 2004. www.washingtonpost.com/wp-dyn/articles/A26784-2004Dec26.html.
2. Quoted in Michael Elliot, "Sea of Sorrow," *Time*, January 10, 2005, p. 22.
3. Quoted in Bay Fang et al. "The Aftermath," *U.S. News & World Report*, January 10, 2005, pp. 10–16.
4. Quoted in Maryann Mott, "Did Animals Sense Tsunami Was Coming?" *National Geographic News*, January 4, 2005. http://news.nationalgeographic.com/news/2005/01/0104_050104_tsunami_animals.html.

Chapter 2: A Raging Wall of Water

5. Daniel Pendick, "A Deadly Force," Savage Earth: *Waves of Destruction: Tsunamis*, PBS Online. www.pbs.org/wnet/savageearth/tsunami.
6. Pendick, "A Deadly Force."

7. Elliott, "Sea of Sorrow," p. 22.
8. Dobbs, "It Seemed Like a Scene from the Bible."
9. Quoted in the Associated Press, "Tsunami Change to Coastlines Likely Temporary," MSNBC, January 4, 2005. www.msnbc.msn.com/id/6786587.

Chapter 3: Disasters of Nature

10. Joseph B. Verrengia, "Earthquakes Still Rearrange Earth After 300 Million Years," *Muskegon Chronicle*, January 9, 2005, p. 6A.
11. Douglas James Gates, "Good Friday Earthquake," The Great Land of Alaska. www.greatlandofalaska.com/reference/GoodFridayQuake.html.
12. Michael Paine, "Asteroids & Tsunamis," Space.com, November 5, 1999. www.space.com/scienceastronomy/astronomy/asteroid_paine_september.html.

Chapter 4: Sounding the Alarm

13. Helen Gibbons, Jennifer Leigh Oates, and Bruce Jaffe, "USGS Scientists Study Sediment Deposited by 2004 Indian Ocean Tsunami," *Sound Waves*, February 2005. http://soundwaves.usgs.gov/2005/02.
14. Quoted in Gibbons, Oates, and Jaffe, "USGS Scientists Study Sediment Deposited by 2004 Indian Ocean Tsunami."

15. Mark Simkin, "Japan Likely to Take Lead in Tsunami Warning System," *Australian Broadcasting System*, January 6, 2005. www.abc.net.au/pm/content/2005/s1277760.htm.

16. Quoted in *World News*, "Tsunami Predicted, Not Heeded," December 30, 2004. www9.sbs.com.au/theworldnews/region.php?id=102025&region=4.

17. Quoted in Will Knight, "Tsunami Warning System Is Not Simply Sensors," *New Scientist.com*, January 4, 2005. www.newscientist.com/article.ns?id=dn6839.

18. Quoted in Julianna Kettlewell, "Tsunami Alert Technology—the Iron Link," *BBC News*, March 25, 2005. http://news.bbc.co.uk/1/hi/sci/tech/4373333.stm.

Glossary

crest: The top of a wave.

epicenter: The point on Earth's surface immediately above where an earthquake is generated.

fault lines (or **faults**): Cracks or breaks in Earth's crust.

inundation: The distance a tsunami travels inland from a coastline.

plate tectonics: The scientific theory that Earth's crust is divided into twelve gigantic chunks known as plates.

Richter scale: The system used to measure an earthquake's magnitude.

run-up: The maximum height of a tsunami.

sediments: Fine particles of soil, sand, and minerals that are deposited in layers by wind and water.

seismic: Refers to shock waves in Earth caused by earthquakes.

seismographs: Instruments that record vibrations in Earth (known as seismic waves).

swell: Ocean waves that travel away from the area where they were generated.

trough: The bottom part of a wave.

tsunami: A series of massive sea waves caused by violent disturbances in Earth.

wave trains: Large chains of waves that make up a tsunami.

wavelength: The distance between the crests of waves.

For Further Exploration

Books

Christy Steele, *Tsunamis*. Austin, TX: Raintree Steck-Vaughn, 2002. A book that discusses what tsunamis are, how they form, and the damage they have done throughout history.

Luke Thompson, *Tsunamis*. New York: Children's, 2000. Offers a variety of facts about tsunamis through real-life stories.

Periodicals

Fiona Bayrock, "Wall of Water," *Yes Mag: Canada's Science Magazine for Kids,* May/June 2004, p. 15.

Internet Sources

National Geographic.com Kids, "Killer Wave! Tsunami." www.nationalgeographic.com/ngkids/9610/kwave/index.html. A collection of information about tsunamis that is colorful as well as interesting.

National Geographic News, "The Deadliest Tsunami in History?" http://news.nationalgeographic.com/news/2004/12/1227_041226_tsunami.html. An article about the December 2004 tsunami and its effects on the people and the land.

Daniel Pendick, "A Deadly Force," Savage Earth: *Waves of Destruction: Tsunamis,* PBS Online.

www.pbs.org/ wnet/savageearth/tsunami. Articles that provide in-depth information about tsunamis. Site includes animated segments so young people can see for themselves how tsunamis form and spread.

Annie Schleicher, "Scientists Explain Origin of South Asia's Deadly Tsunamis," *NewsHour Extra,* December 30, 2004. www.pbs.org/newshour/extra/ features/july-dec04/tsunami_12-30.html.

Time for Kids, Special Report: Asia's Tsunami. www.timeforkids.com/TFK/specials/articles/ 0,6709,1013398,00.html. An excellent, comprehensive collection of articles on the December 26, 2004, tsunami in Indonesia. The site also includes an animated movie.

Web Sites

How Stuff Works (www.howstuffworks.com). Includes several detailed sections related to tsunamis, including "How Tsunamis Work" and "How Earthquakes Work."

Tsunamis and Earthquakes, U.S. Geological Survey (USGS) (http://walrus.wr.usgs.gov/tsunami). A comprehensive site that includes information on how tsunamis are generated, as well as virtual reality models of tsunamis and summaries of research studies. Colorful animations help tell the story.

Index

Picture Credits

About the Author

Peggy J. Parks holds a bachelor of science degree from Aquinas College in Grand Rapids, Michigan, where she graduated magna cum laude. She has written more than 40 titles for Thomson Gale's KidHaven Press, Blackbirch Press, and Lucent Books imprints, and has written and self-published her own cookbook. Parks lives in Muskegon, Michigan, a town she says inspires her writing because of its location on the shores of Lake Michigan.